## Prayer Journal for Older Women:

### An Inspirational Journal with Bible Verses, Motivational Quotes, Prayer Prompts and Spaces for Reflections

**From the Author of the Book, "I'm Loving My Age: A Believer's Guide to Aging Gracefully and Words of Hope for the Elderly"**

Prayer Journal for Women

© 2021 Andrea Clarke Pratt

All rights reserved. No portion of this book may be reproduced in any form without permission from the publisher, except as permitted by U.S. copyright law. For permissions contact: adpratt6@gmail.com

Unless otherwise indicated, Scripture quotations taken from the King James Version (KJV) - public domain.

This Prayer Journal
Belongs To

# Suggested Prayer Points

- Prayer of Adoration
- Prayer of Praise and Thanksgiving
- Prayer for Israel
- Prayer for Religious Leaders
- Prayer for Governmental Leaders and Other Persons in Authority
- Prayer for your Nation and Government
- Prayer for Africa, Antarctica, Asia, Australia/Oceania, Europe, North America, and South America
- Prayer for Missions
- Prayer for Current Global Issues
- Prayer for those who are Persecuted because of the Gospel
- Prayer for the Hungry, Abused and Oppressed
- Prayer for Revival
- Prayer for your Family
- Prayer for your Local Church
- Prayer for the Global Church
- Prayer for Forgiveness and Repentance
- Prayer for Spiritual Insight, Wisdom, and your Walk with God
- Prayer for your Physical Needs
- Prayer for Deliverance from Evil
- Prayer for Women All Around the World

# Scripture Text of the Week

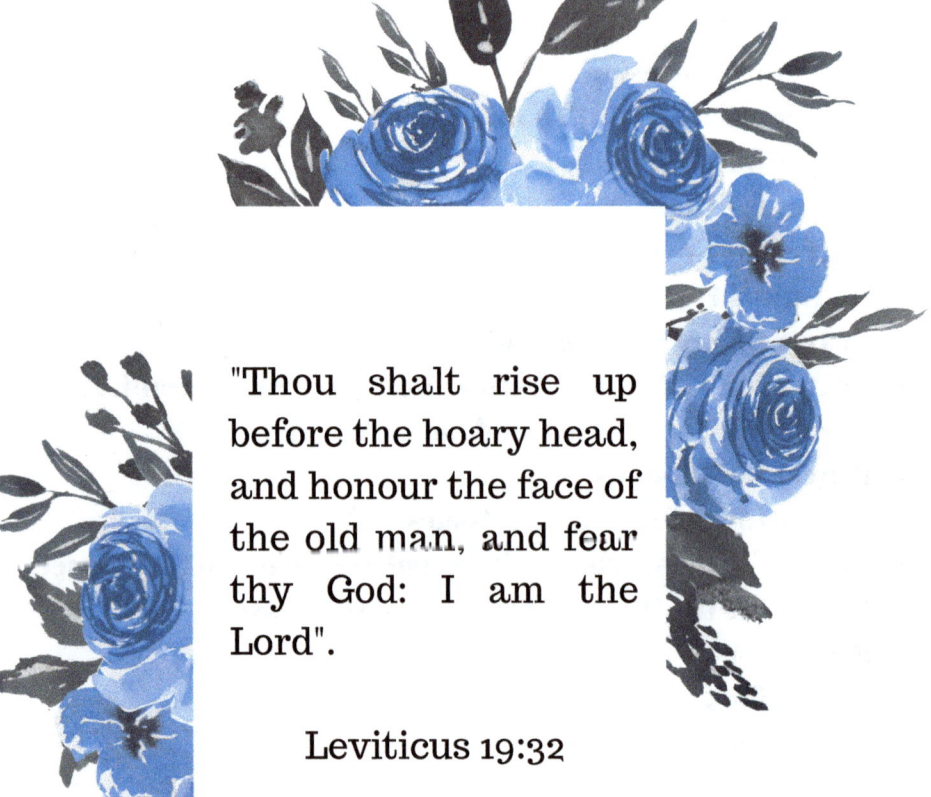

"Thou shalt rise up before the hoary head, and honour the face of the old man, and fear thy God: I am the Lord".

Leviticus 19:32

# Quote of the Week

"We can complain because rose bushes have thorns, or rejoice because thorn bushes have roses..."

Abraham Lincoln

ACTS

# Adoration

### Give God praise and honor for who He is

"Thou art worthy, O Lord, to receive glory and honour and power: for thou hast created all things, and for thy pleasure they are and were created" (Revelations 4:11).

_____
_____
_____
_____
_____

# Confession

### Confess your sins to God

"If we confess our sins, He is Faithful and Just to forgive us our sins and to cleanse us from all unrighteousness" (1 John 1:9).

_____
_____
_____
_____
_____

# Thanksgiving

### Thank God for all of the blessings He has given to you.

**"O give thanks unto the Lord; for he is good: for his mercy endureth for ever" (Psalms 136:1).**

_____
_____
_____
_____
_____

# Supplication

### Pray for your needs and the needs of others

**"Be careful for nothing; but in every thing by prayer and supplication with thanksgiving let your requests be made known unto God"
(Philippians 4:6).**

_____
_____
_____
_____
_____

**Date:**_____

## *My Prayer Focus for Today*

## *Lord I am Grateful for*

## *Today I Will Pray for the Following Persons*

# My Prayer

"I will praise thee; for I am fearfully and wonderfully made: marvelous are thy works; and that my soul knoweth right well" (Psalm 139:14).

**Date:**_____

## My Prayer Focus for Today

## Lord I am Grateful for

## Today I Will Pray for the Following Persons

# My Prayer

"When my soul fainted within me I remembered the LORD: and my prayer came in unto thee, into thine holy temple" (Jonah 2:7).

**Date:** _____

## My Prayer Focus for Today

## Lord I am Grateful for

## Today I Will Pray for the Following Persons

# My Prayer

"She is more precious than rubies: and all the things thou canst desire are not to be compared unto her". (Proverbs 3:15-18)

**Date:**_____

## My Prayer Focus for Today

### Lord I am Grateful for

### Today I Will Pray for the Following Persons

# My Prayer

"In my distress I called upon the Lord, and cried unto my God: he heard my voice out of his temple, and my cry came before him, even into his ears" (Psalm 18:6).

**Date:**_____

## My Prayer Focus for Today

## Lord I am Grateful for

## Today I Will Pray for the Following Persons

# My Prayer

"The aged women likewise, that they be in behaviour as becometh holiness, not false accusers, not given to much wine, teachers of good things" (Titus 2:3-5).

**Date:**_____

## *My Prayer Focus for Today*

### *Lord I am Grateful for*

### *Today I Will Pray for the Following Persons*

**Date:**_____

### My Prayer Focus for Today

### Lord I am Grateful for

### Today I Will Pray for the Following Persons

# My Prayer

"Strength and honour are her clothing;
and she shall rejoice in time to come."
(Proverbs 31:25)

# Scripture Text of the Week

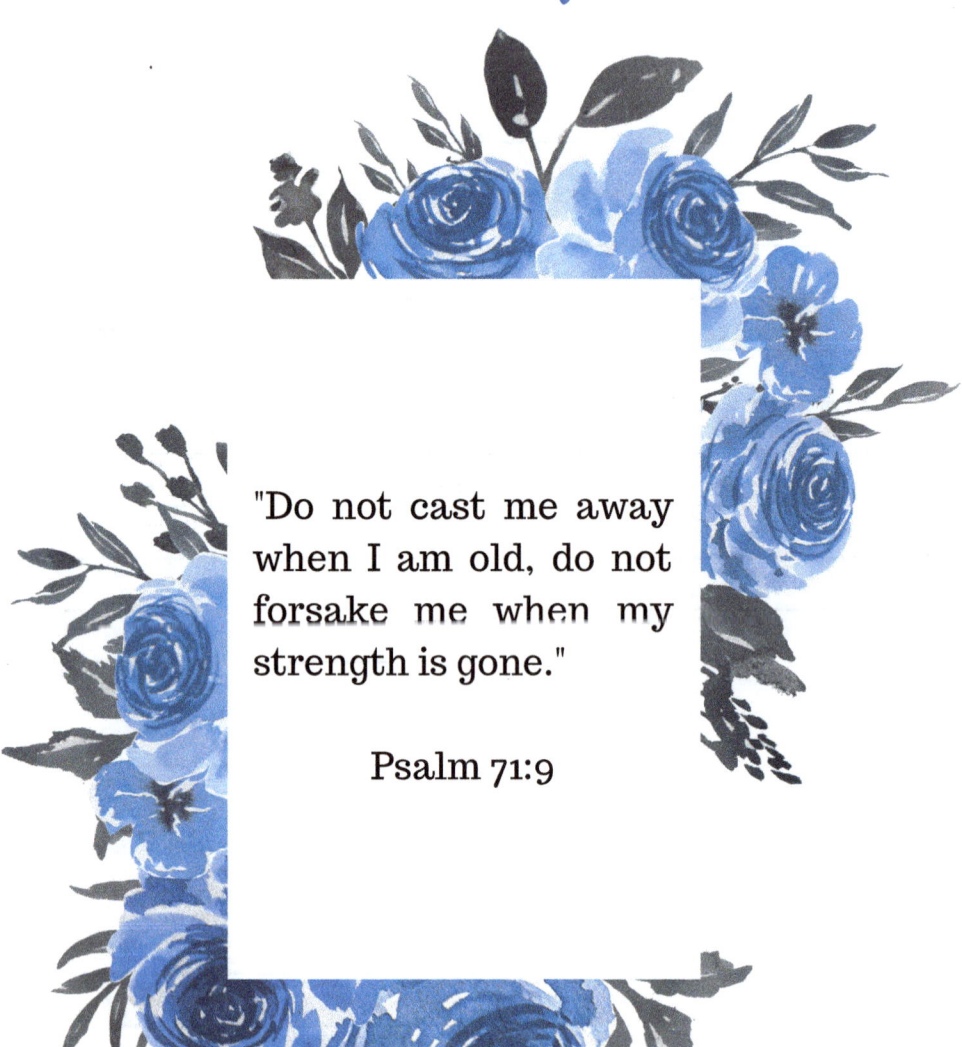

"Do not cast me away when I am old, do not forsake me when my strength is gone."

Psalm 71:9

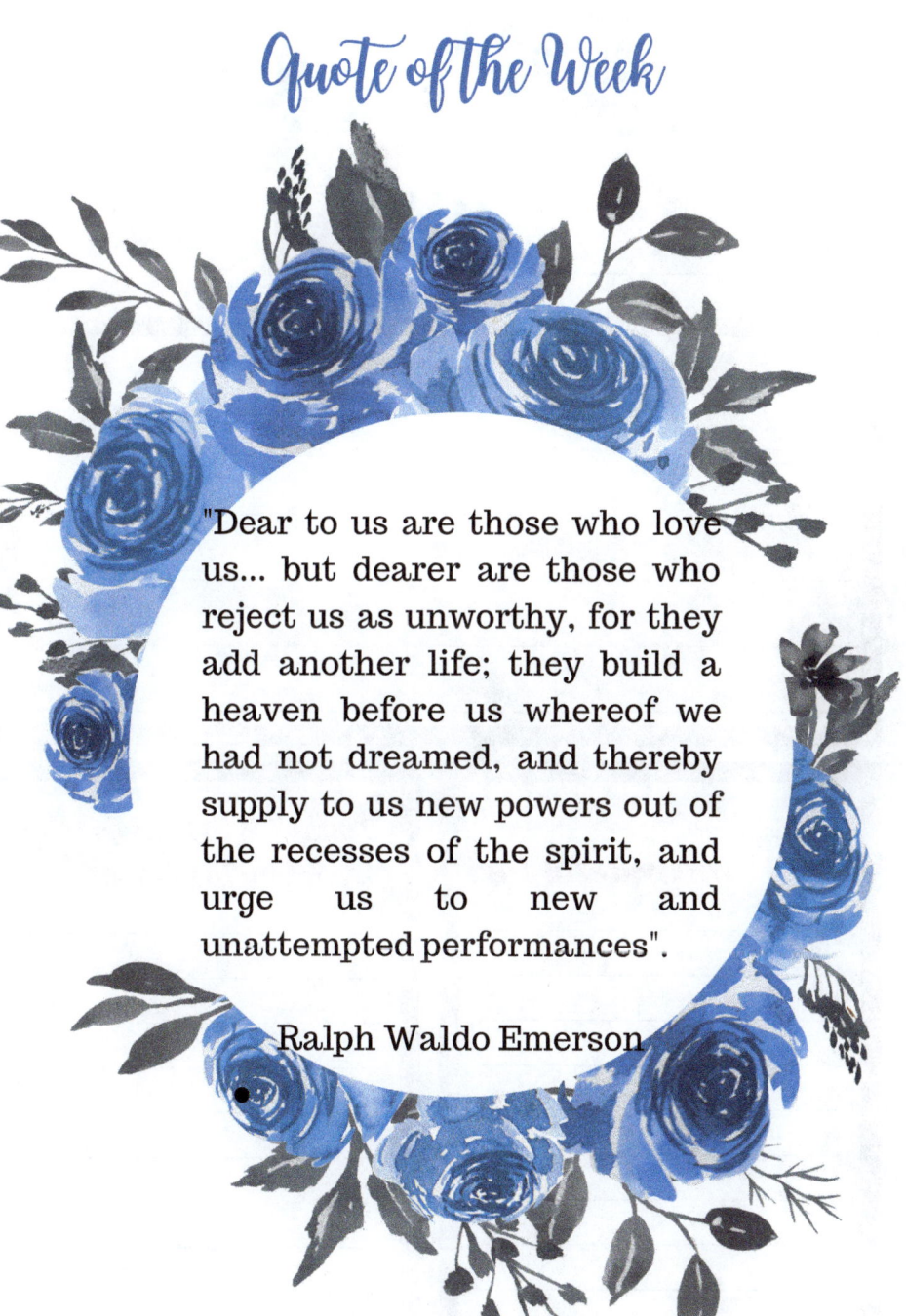

# Quote of the Week

"Dear to us are those who love us... but dearer are those who reject us as unworthy, for they add another life; they build a heaven before us whereof we had not dreamed, and thereby supply to us new powers out of the recesses of the spirit, and urge us to new and unattempted performances".

Ralph Waldo Emerson

**Date:**_____

## My Prayer Focus for Today

## Lord I am Grateful for

## Today I Will Pray for the Following Persons

# My Prayer

"What shall we then say to these things?
If God be for us, who can be against us"?
(Romans 8:31).

**Date:**_____

## *My Prayer Focus for Today*

### Lord I am Grateful for

### Today I Will Pray for the Following Persons

# My Prayer

"Who can find a virtuous woman? for her price is far above rubies."

**(Proverbs 31:10-31)**

**Date:**_____

### My Prayer Focus for Today

### Lord I am Grateful for

### Today I Will Pray for the Following Persons

# My Prayer

"Wait on the Lord. Be of good courage and he shall strengthen thine heart: wait, I say, on the Lord" (Psalm 27:14).

**Date:**_____

## My Prayer Focus for Today

### Lord I am Grateful for

### Today I Will Pray for the Following Persons

# My Prayer

"Favour is deceitful, and beauty is vain: but a woman that feareth the LORD, she shall be praised" (Proverbs 31:30-31).

**Date:**_____

## *My Prayer Focus for Today*

## *Lord I am Grateful for*

## *Today I Will Pray for the Following Persons*

**Date:**_____

## *My Prayer Focus for Today*

### *Lord I am Grateful for*

### *Today I Will Pray for the Following Persons*

# My Prayer

*"God is in the midst of her; she shall not be moved: God shall help her, and that right early (Psalms 16:5).*

**Date:**_____

### My Prayer Focus for Today

### Lord I am Grateful for

### Today I Will Pray for the Following Persons

# My Prayer

*"God is in the midst of her; she shall not be moved: God shall help her, and that right early (Psalms 16:5).*

# Scripture Text of the Week

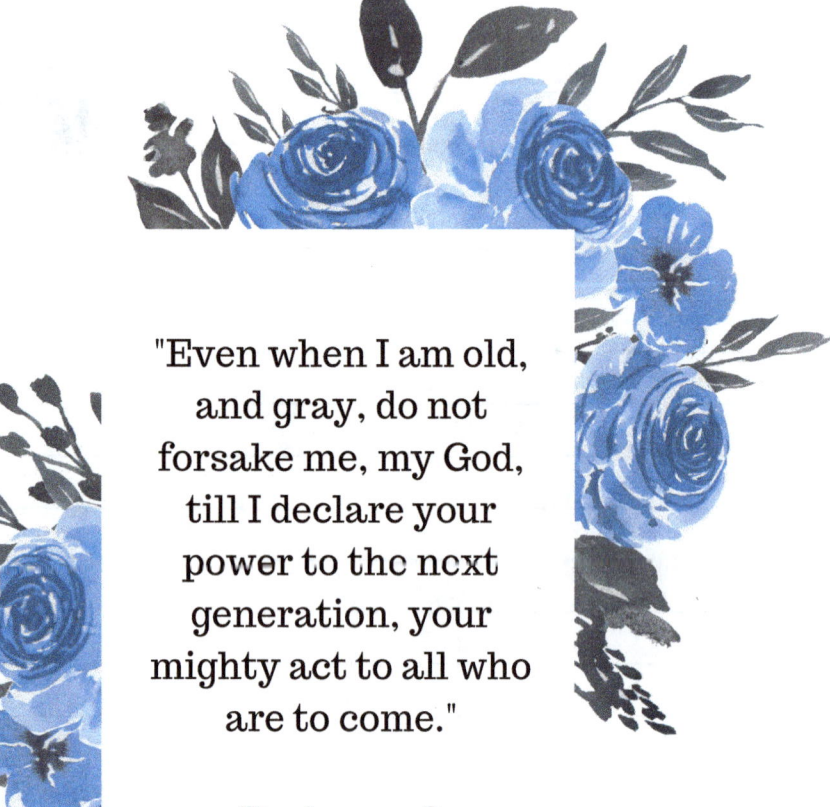

"Even when I am old, and gray, do not forsake me, my God, till I declare your power to the next generation, your mighty act to all who are to come."

Psalm 71:18

# Quote of the Week

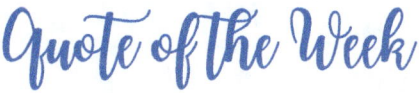

"As I grow older, I pay less attention to what men say. I just watch what they do. "

Andrew Carnegie

**Date:**_____

## My Prayer Focus for Today

### Lord I am Grateful for

### Today I Will Pray for the Following Persons

# My Prayer

"My voice shalt thou hear in the morning, O LORD; in the morning will I direct [my prayer] unto thee, and will look up" (Psalms 5:3).

**Date:**_____

## My Prayer Focus for Today

## Lord I am Grateful for

## Today I Will Pray for the Following Persons

# My Prayer

"She openeth her mouth with wisdom;
and in her tongue is the law of kindness"
(Proverbs 31:26)

**Date:**_____

## My Prayer Focus for Today

### Lord I am Grateful for

### Today I Will Pray for the Following Persons

# My Prayer

"She rises also while it is still night And gives food to her household and portions to her maidens" (Proverbs 31:15).

**Date:**_____

## My Prayer Focus for Today

### Lord I am Grateful for

### Today I Will Pray for the Following Persons

# My Prayer

"Honor thou father and thy mother: that thy days may be long upon the land which the Lord thy God giveth thee" (Exodus 20:12).

**Date:**_____

## My Prayer Focus for Today

### Lord I am Grateful for

### Today I Will Pray for the Following Persons

# My Prayer

"He giveth power to the faint; and to them that have no might he increaseth strength" (Isaiah 40:29).

**Date:**_____

## *My Prayer Focus for Today*

### *Lord I am Grateful for*

### *Today I Will Pray for the Following Persons*

# My Prayer

"Even the youths shall faint and be weary, and the young men shall utterly fall: but they that wait upon the lord shall renew their strenght:"
Isaiah 40:30-31

**Date:**_____

## *My Prayer Focus for Today*

### *Lord I am Grateful for*

### *Today I Will Pray for the Following Persons*

# My Prayer

"My flesh and my heart faileth, but God is the strength of my heart and my portion forever" (Psalm 73:26).

 # Notes

# Notes

# Notes

 # Notes

## About the Author

Andrea Clarke Pratt retired in 2018 after more than 30 years in the corporate world. She then pursued the field of Education and is currently teaching at a High School. Her hunger for the Word of God led her to complete a Master's Degree in Theology.

Andrea is also the Author of the book ***"I'm Loving My Age: A Believer's Guide to Aging Gracefully and Words of Hope for the Elderly"***. The book is a compilation of promises from the Bible, poems on aging, legacy statements, and even a family tree that encourages its older readers to celebrate all the wisdom and insight they have acquired over the years and help them realize that age is not something to be looked down upon. The older generation can still be used by God to awaken everyone, including the younger generation, to what it means to know and love Jesus.

Contact:

adpratt6@gmail.com

CPSIA information can be obtained
at www.ICGtesting.com
Printed in the USA
LVHW060152150921
697853LV00009B/183